Published by Gallery Books
A Division of W H Smith Publishers Inc.
112 Madison Avenue
New York, New York 10016

Produced by
Brompton Books Corp.
15 Sherwood Place
Greenwich, CT 06830

Copyright © 1990 Brompton Books Corp.

ISBN 0-8317-8691-4

Printed in Hong Kong

10 9 8 7 6 5 4 3 2 1

TEXAS

TEXT	FRANK MOLLICA
DESIGN	ADRIAN HODGKINS

GALLERY BOOKS
An imprint of W.H. Smith Publishers Inc.
112 Madison Avenue
New York, New York 10016

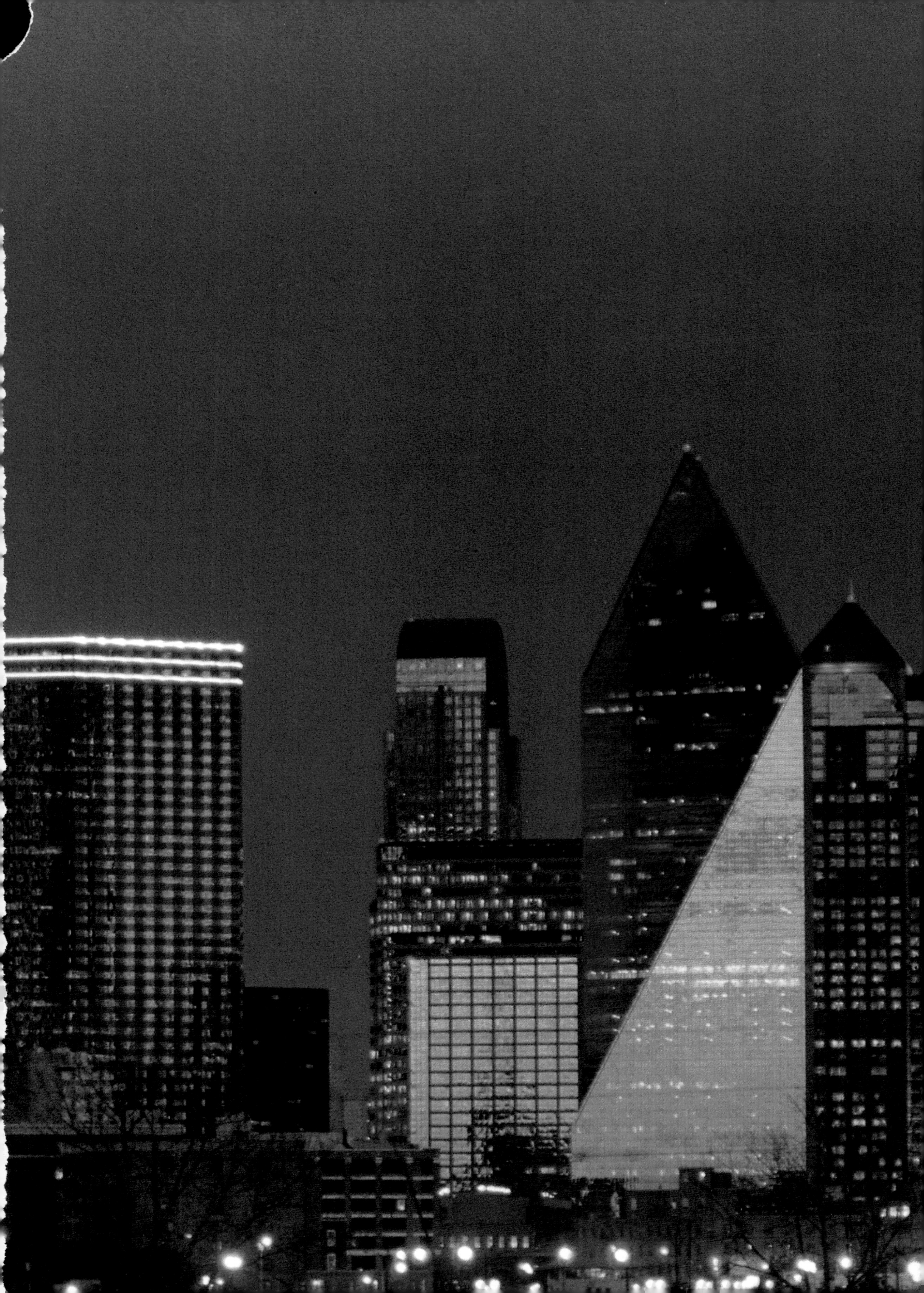

3/6 The impressive Dallas skyline at night.

INTRODUCTION

In 1519, the land we now call Texas was inhabited solely by Indians. Over the next 350 years, however, it would exist under six different flags and undergo the diverse experiences that laid the foundation for the Texas of the twentieth century and of popular imagination. Spanish and Mexican rule would play a large role in the region's history and in the development of today's Texas. The time-honored images that emerged from this era have become known around the world.

A visitor to Texas in 1890 would have found a culture and a way of life very similar to that which lives on in legends today: cowboys and Indians, ranches as large as nations, endless railroads, mountains, and plains. Today's visitor, on the other hand, will find a Texas very different from that of 100 years ago. Now it is one of the most diverse of American states. While images of the old-time Texas endure, people also see the state as a microcosm of the nation, with a diverse ethnic composition, a varied economy, and land that ranges from arid plains to coastal marshlands and islands.

Texas' diversity can be attributed largely to the state's great size. Except for Alaska, Texas is the largest of all the states and encompasses several different topographic regions and climates. One could drive in a straight line for close to 1000 miles without leaving the state, and discover the many climatic and geographic regions that make Texas unique: the Great Plains, hardwood forests, endless fields of wildflowers, mountains rising from desert sands, and the Gulf Coast and the National Seashore. The land is inhabited by hundreds of different species of plants and animals, from cactus and rattlesnakes to evergreens and deer. This natural beauty has attracted thousands of tourists to Texas, not only from other states, but also from around the world. Big Bend National Park and Aransas National Wildlife Refuge are two of the state's many natural treasures. The Highland Lakes run right through the capital city of Austin. The result of manmade dams, they provide a beautiful natural setting. The islands of the Gulf Coast, with their spotless beaches and excellent sport fishing, attract many visitors.

The differing regions of Texas also provide the state with a wealth of economic interests. Ranching and oil are two of the best known. These industries are active all over the state, which leads the nation in beef and oil production. Such crops as cotton and rice are also important to the state's economy, as are poultry and dairy products. Texas also has large quantities of helium and natural gas, the extraction of which has become a major industry. The Gulf Coast contributes to the economy by providing deep-water ports, including Houston, which is one of the nation's largest. Through these ports, Texas can export many of the vital commodities that it produces. The coast is also a major commercial fishing center, for shrimp and other seafoods.

Houston, Dallas-Forth Worth, and Austin are among the leading metropolitan areas in the state and the nation. In addition to its mammoth shipping industry, Houston is a leader in aerospace research and the site of NASA's Manned Space Center. Dallas has become a leader in the service industry because of its major international banking system. Fort Worth is a hard-working historic city prominent in the cattle industry, thanks to the Fort Worth Stockyards. Austin's main business is government, but the city is also the site of the main branch of the University of Texas and is a center for high-tech electronics research and manufacturing.

The urbanization of Texas, including a movement in population from rural to urban areas, has also widened the state's range of cultural activities. Dallas has been a cultural center since the 1800s; today it has both an international flavor and a dazzling nightlife. Cultural attractions include the theater, symphony, art exhibits, and the world-famous Dallas Opera. Museums with themes from both past and present can be found in most Texas cities. The Kennedy Historic Exhibit in Dallas is an important piece of the nation's history. San Antonio's beautiful River Walk inspires visitors to relax and enjoy a delightful holiday. And Galveston's Mardis Gras is a reminder that Texas, especially its Gulf Coast, owes much to Southern tradition.

Although lifestyles in Texas have changed during the twentieth century, one cannot forget what is perhaps the state's richest treasure—its history. When Texas was discovered and explored by the Spanish in the early sixteenth century, little was done for its long-range development. But when the French showed interest in the territory, the Spanish government became more active, and Spanish-French relations dominated the region's history for 300 years. Then, in 1821, American Moses Austin obtained a grant of land from the Mexican government, which had recently expelled the Spanish. He planned to settle 300 families in the first American colony in Texas. His son Stephen Austin carried out this plan after his father's death, convincing the new Mexican government to allow orderly colonization. The capital of Texas now bears his name. Within 15 years, 20,000 settlers had entered

Texas from the United States, Europe and Mexico, bringing with them 4000 black slaves. Today, a quarter of the state's population is either black or Mexican.

By 1836, however, the colonists had become disenchanted with the Mexican government and its military dictator, Santa Anna. The infamous battle at the Alamo would result from the formation of a small "war party" on behalf of the Texans. The battle was a disaster for the Americans, but it served as an inspiration for the rest of the rebellion. The phrase "Remember the Alamo" has become one of the best-known war cries in the world. The settlers' tenacity led them to victory over the Mexicans within the year, and the establishment of the Republic of Texas, with Sam Houston as its president, soon followed. Although the Republic lasted only a short time before it joined the United States, Texas remains the only state ever to have been an independent republic.

This frontier Texas is the one that gave rise to most of the tall tales, and it was, indeed, a rough land that required a rugged way of life. The settlers did not enjoy the comforts of civilization that were long established in the East. This is one reason why the "typical" Texan is known to be hardy and self-reliant. Another reason for this reputation comes from the influence of Spanish and Mexican rule. In Spanish and Hispanic cultures, the ideal of *machismo*—aggressive masculinity—is dominant. One who embodies this quality is considered a leader, endowed with physical and moral strength. He is charismatic, with a sense of duty and honor to those who depend on him. This ideal of *machismo* may explain the attraction of the Texan image:

cowboys herding cattle on the open range and brave pioneers settling an arid frontier. Colorful figures like Judge Roy Bean, the "Law West of the Pecos," have helped keep the legend alive.

Immigration, modernization, and the passage of time have eroded many of these characteristics, but to call someone a "Texan" still evokes the old way of life. Life on the ranch is not as rough as it once was, but cowboys still run the show, and livestock is essential to the economy. Rodeos are as rough as ever, and Texas has become famous for them. In Ciudad Juarez, the Mexican sister city of El Paso, bullfights are held regularly. Other events include the Chisholm Trail Roundup, and pioneer museums are scattered throughout the state, especially in the south and west. Many Spanish missions still stand as a reminder of the early days of exploration, and other historic sites have been restored, including Fort Davis and Fort Bliss. The Tigua Indian Reservation in northwest Texas is a living reminder of the importance of the Indian population to Texas' history.

The associations that people often make when they hear the name "Texas" do not always do justice to what the state is today, and what it has to offer. Although much of Texas is still rural, its cities are flourishing. Urbanization has brought increased immigration and helped the state become an international center for business, finance, travel, high-tech research, and much more. Texans take pride in all these things—the same pride they take in their history and in their many fine athletic programs. The pages that follow capture a glimpse of the beauty and diversity of the Lone Star State—Texas.

NORTHEAST AND CENTRAL

The diversity of Northeast and Central Texas reflects that of the state as a whole. The topography is similar throughout the region—primarily level ground with gently sloping hills. In the east, however, the land resembles the Deep South, with a mixture of swamps and dense pine forests. The land in the east is fertile, and, as in the rest of the South, cotton is an important crop, although rice has become dominant in recent years. The entire state of Texas has been blessed with productive oil fields, and east Texas is no exception. Oil is important here, as are the pine forests, which support a lumber industry.

The swamps and pine forests of the east give way to prairie grassland and oak in central Texas. The land is well-suited to raising cattle and such crops as cotton and fruit. The region's climate is quite temperate and supports a wide variety of wildlife, including many deer. The Blackland Prairie lies just outside of Dallas and provides a congenial environment for both animals and people. Seemingly endless fields of bluebonnets and other wildflowers are a welcome sight, where quiet replaces the bustle of the nearby city.

Rising from this prairie is the "supercity" of Dallas-Forth Worth. The metropolitan area of these two cities accounts for almost one-quarter of the state's population. Forth Worth is still very much a lively cattle town. Down-to-earth and hard-working, Fort Worth remains a major component of Texas' vast cattle industry. In Dallas, extravagance is the rule, and commerce is the major industry. Indirectly, Dallas controls much of the state and is an international player in industries, from aerospace and oil to finance and insurance. Well-equipped to show visitors a good time, Dallas boasts a nightlife that includes everything from opera to cosmopolitan nightclubs, superior restaurants and numerous luxury hotels. Rodeos are popular, but "America's team," the Dallas Cowboys, still rules the sports arena, followed by baseball's up-and-coming Texas Rangers, who hail from Arlington, between Dallas and Forth Worth.

15 The Reunion Tower and skyscrapers of the Dallas skyline tower over the surrounding prairie. Texas' second largest city is home to international business as well as a cosmopolitan nightlife.

16/17 The Dallas Infomart world trade center is located within the Dallas Market Center complex, which covers over 150 acres in the downtown area.

18/19 Located in Arlington, Six Flags Over Texas theme park is a testament to the pride that Texans have in their unique history under six nations.

20 One of the facilities of State Fair Park, the
Cotton Bowl plays host to the NCAA's annual
New Year's contest as well as the Texas-
Oklahoma football game, one of college foot-
ball's biggest rivalries.

21 Tony Dorsett, the NFL's second all-time leading rusher, became the pride of the Dallas Cowboys during the late 1970s and early 1980s, when they earned their title of "America's Team."

22/23 The home of the Dallas Aquarium, Museum of Natural History, and the Cotton Bowl, State Fair Park hosts the Texas State Fair every October.

24/25 Dealy Plaza in Dallas, the site of John F Kennedy's assassination, is now the home of the Kennedy Memorial Center (right).

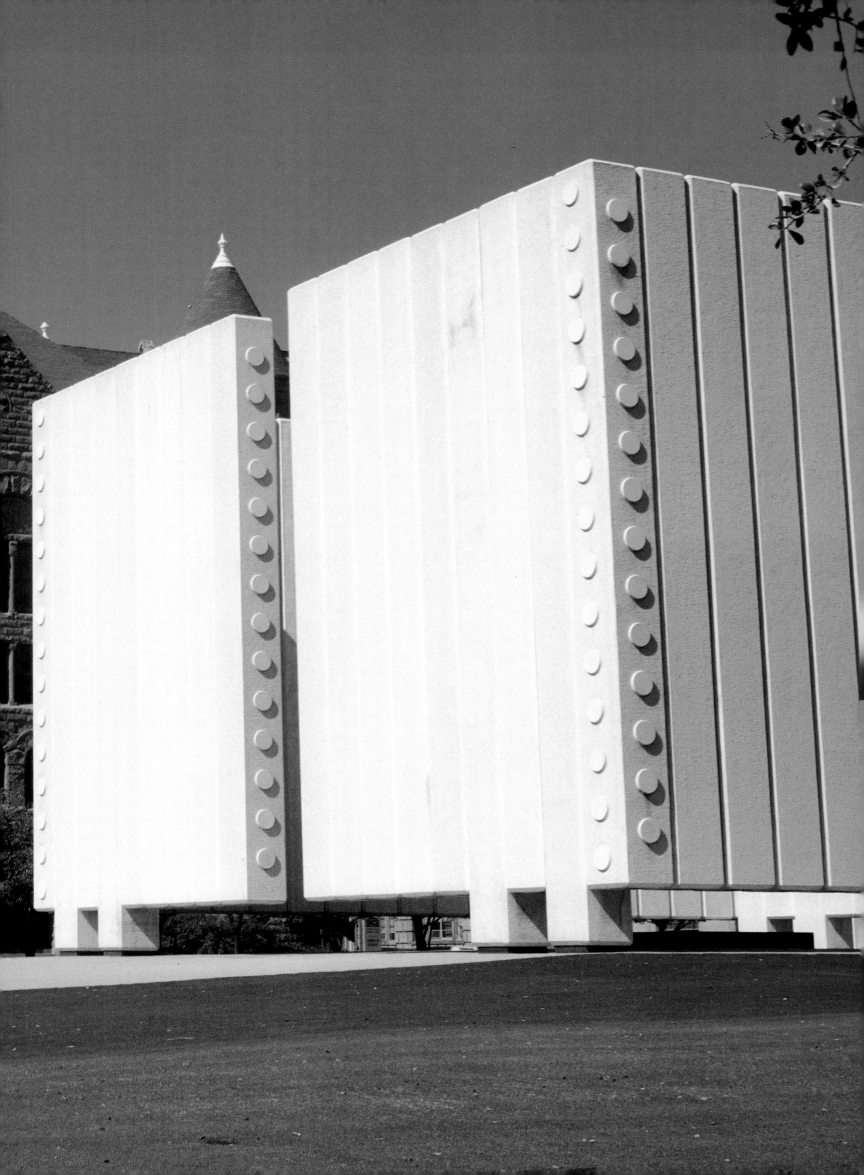

28 The Southwestern Exposition and Livestock Show parade in downtown Fort Worth celebrates the industry that helped transform the city from a military garrison into a thriving cattle town.

26/27 Fort Worth, the largest livestock center in the Southwest, dominates the night sky in a spectacle of brilliant light. In contrast to its sister city, Dallas, Forth Worth retains the atmosphere of a frontier town.

29 Cattle being driven in the Fort Worth Stockyards. After the Civil War, the presence of the stockyards around Fort Worth caused the city to become a major shipping point, which later helped to facilitate Texas' growing oil industry.

30/31 This mural of the Chisholm Trail in Fort Worth captures the ruggedness of both the cowboys and the Texas Longhorn. The Chisholm Trail was heavily travelled for ten years until it was declared off-limits by Kansas farmers.

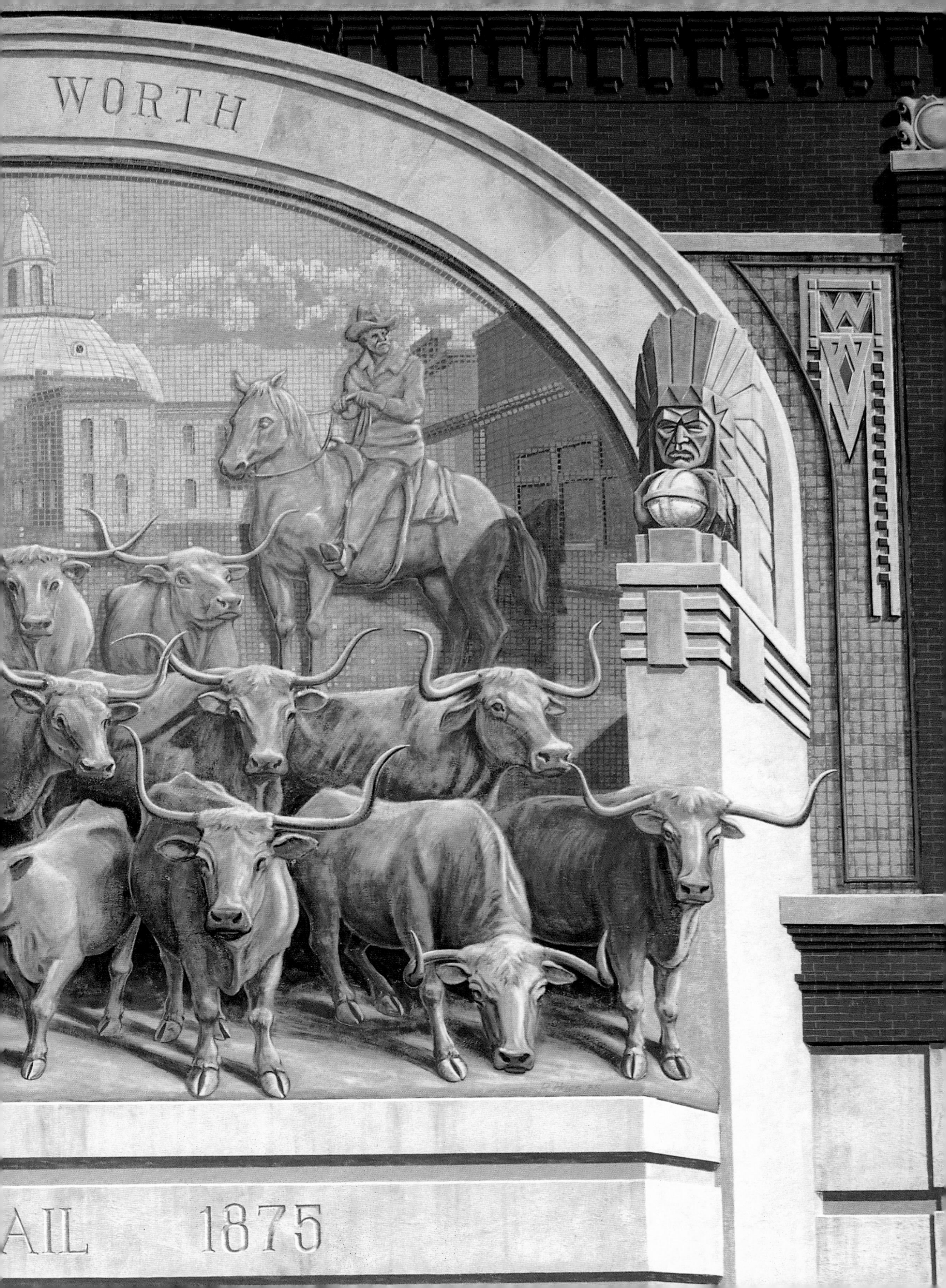
WORTH
AIL 1875

32/33 Wildflowers blanket a field in the Blackland Prairie, an area of northeast Texas characterized by gently sloping hills, fertile soil, and numerous species of plants and wildlife.

34 Texas A & M University, founded in 1876, has been a pioneer in agricultural engineering as well as aerospace technology.

35 The Waxahachie Courthouse, in Ellis County, displays its remarkable architectural style.

36 The beautiful Tyler Rose Garden in east Texas is one of the many public gardens which decorate the state and provide a relaxing retreat for both residents and visitors alike.

37 When first opened, the suspension bridge crossing the Brazos River at Waco was the longest single span suspension bridge in the United States and the second longest in the world.

38/39 The mangrove swamps of Caddo Lake in east Texas are evidence of the ties that this area has with the Deep South.

40 The town of Navasota still looks much as it did
when it became the center of the cotton industry
in Texas about 100 years ago.

41 Texas is, surprisingly, the nation's leader in cotton production. Much of the state's production is centered in the north and central regions of the state.

THE GULF COAST

The Gulf Coast region of Texas extends for more than 350 miles along the Gulf of Mexico and as much as 50 miles inland. As a state of mind, however, the Gulf Coast has a wider influence. Along the actual coastline and on the nearby islands, the atmosphere is relaxed and the beaches are among the most beautiful in the country. The area is a popular vacation spot that has everything necessary to keep its visitors happy: a wide variety of watersports, excellent sportfishing, boating, and sandy beaches. A tropical climate makes the Gulf Coast a natural wildlife refuge, home to many colorful species of migratory birds. Although the same weather that welcomes wildlife is also conducive to tropical storms, the islands that run parallel to the coast for most of its length provide an effective buffer for the mainland. The most notable of these are Padre Island, Mustang Island, and Galveston. These islands are supported mainly by tourism and commercial fishing, and Galveston is especially active. The Galveston Island Shrimp Festival, which celebrates the island's major catch, and its Mardi Gras, which reflects the festive atmosphere of the region, attract many visitors annually.

In the larger cities and towns along the coast, one of the major industries is commercial shipping. This is facilitated by 15 deep-water ports and 15 shallower ports, and by the natural ship channel provided by the offshore islands. Oil can be found in this region, and rice is the major crop. Oil refineries and chemical plants are a common sight on the skylines of the larger cities. The shipping industry of the region supports the others by providing them with raw materials and by serving as a conduit for their products.

Houston is the population center of the region, with its huge shipping and refining interests, and the city's economy and character are diversified by other industries such as aerospace technology. The presence of NASA's Manned Space Center makes Houston a major site for the nation's space program. The spirited people of Houston are its most valuable commodity, and that pride and intensity shows in their support for their sports teams—the Oilers, the Rockets, and the Astros.

The Gulf Coast as a whole is much more than a seaside resort or a sprawling metropolis. The region's history is typically Texan: innovative, enterprising, and tenacious.

43 A gorgeous sunset silhouettes the Point Bolivar lighthouse in Galveston, on the subtropical Gulf Coast.

44/45 Houston is the largest and fastest-growing city in the Southwest. Houston's shipping and transportation are the backbone of many of the state's industries.

46/47 In addition to such production industries as oil, Houston also leads the Southwest in retail sales volume and is a center for industrial marketing and commercial banking.

48 Akeem Olajuwon (34) of the Houston Rockets goes up for two points against the Chicago Bulls. The Rockets are just one of the successful college and pro teams that call Houston their home.

49 The Astros play before an enthusiastic crowd in the Houston Astrodome, one of the city's most impressive structures. The complex can seat as many as 66,000 and was at one time the largest covered sports arena in the world.

50/51 NASA's Manned Space Center, on the outskirts of Houston, has made the city a major center for aerospace technology in the United States.

52/53 An oil refinery near Houston is thrown into relief by the sunset. The Houston area is one of the densest regions of oil production in the country.

54 Originally launched in 1877 and restored by
the Galveston Historical Society, Elissa is typical
of the ships that helped to establish Gulf Coast
ports like Galveston.

55 One of the larger harbor towns on the Gulf Coast, Corpus Christi also makes a living through such diversified pursuits as oil production and space-age technology.

56 A shrimper decorated for the Galveston Island Shrimp Festival. The Festival is a celebration of the island's main catch and attracts a large number of tourists, another big source of income on the island.

57 Neptune is an appropriate subject for a float in Galveston's Mardis Gras parade. The jubilant atmosphere of the island during the event symbolizes the greater connection between this area of Texas and the entire Gulf Coast region.

58/59 The Gulf Coast of Texas is a popular resort destination during the summer months. Here, enthusiastic beachgoers prepare to enjoy a beautiful day with an assortment of colorful catamarans and windsurfers.

60/61 Palm trees line a street in Galveston's historically rich Landmark District.

62 The Sidbury House in Corpus Christi was built in 1893. The Texas Historical Society is particularly active along the Gulf Coast.

63 The interior of the Opera House on the Strand in Galveston has been carefully preserved. The area has both an active business district as well as numerous historical sites and buildings.

64/65 Padre Island, the longest of the islands paralleling the coastal mainland of Texas, ranges in width from several hundred yards to three miles and is a favorite spot for vacationers.

66 A Great Blue Heron at Aransas National Wildlife Refuge, on St. Joseph and Mud islands.

67 *A view of the unusual coastline at Aransas. In addition to migratory birds, one can also find species of wildlife as diverse as alligator and deer within the confines of the Refuge.*

68/69 *A fisherman casts a net in the late afternoon sun near Corpus Christi. Sportfishing is popular all along Texas' Gulf Coast.*

THE SOUTHWEST

Southwest Texas is home to the state's capital, as well as the state's origins and a large portion of its history. The land of the southwest is dry and dusty, giving the region its rugged character. Its appearance and atmosphere are reminiscent of the time when the land was still a frontier and transient cowboys were a common sight.

Many of the Spanish missions that once dotted the frontier still stand as a reminder of Texas' colonial heritage. Also in this part of the state the Austins began Texas' first American settlement by leading 300 families to start new lives along the Brazos River. Soon after their settlement, however, the pioneers found reason to be disappointed with their Mexican rulers and they waged a war of independence. When the Republic of Texas was established at the war's end, Austin was named the capital and Sam Houston the president. The most famous battle of that war, and indeed of Texas' entire history, was fought at the Alamo, which remains a symbol of the courage and determination that are typical of Texas.

Today the scenery is much the same as it was in the days of the Republic. With the exception of a few large cities like Austin and San Antonio, the region consists mostly of small scattered towns. A legacy of Spanish and Mexican rule, many communities are bilingual. And the fact that Texas and Mexico are separated here only by the Rio Grande results in frequent interaction across the border.

While many aspects of the southwest remain constant, its economy has become diversified and the city of Austin, in particular, has modernized. Sheep, and beef and dairy cattle, still graze in parts of the southwest. Some oil is extracted, but extensive irrigation has provided the biggest change, turning the once semi-arid region into a productive fruit and vegetable center. Austin conducts its affairs of state from gracious settings like the Capitol building, modeled after its prototype in Washington, D.C. The University of Texas at Austin makes it the educational center of the state and a stimulating sports city as well, since the University has one of the nation's finest collegiate athletic programs.

71 The Mission San Juan Capistrano, erected in 1731, is one of several near San Antonio which date back to the days of Texas' exploration and early settlement.

72 The San Elizario Presidio Chapel was begun in 1877 and was the fourth chapel erected in San Elizario, once the seat of El Paso County.

73 The Chapel Nuestra Senora de Loreto Presidio, better known as the Presidio La Bahia, stands imposingly near present-day Goliad and has been the most fought-over location in the history of Texas.

74/75 The beautiful San José Mission in San Antonio, built in 1768, originally served as a fortified church for the Spanish.

76 San Antonio's River Walk provides a quick es-
cape from the bustle of Texas' third largest city.
Meandering through the center of town for elev-
en blocks, the Walk provides relaxation during
the day and at night, when the route comes to
life in a dazzling display of light.

77 Spanish dancers in San Antonio. One of the oldest cities in Texas, its history as a Spanish outpost and later an American frontier town has given San Antonio a character that is wholly unique.

78 Burro Bluffs, a dramatic stretch of the U.S.-Mexican border along the Rio Grande.

79 Irrigation from the Rio Grande has converted the Magic Valley from a desert to a productive citrus fruit growing region and a valuable part of the Texas economy.

80/81 Clouds gather over this picturesque cattle ranch between Brenham and Columbus. Ranching has been a traditional Texan way of life since the days of the Chisholm Trail and is still widespread throughout much of the state.

82 The State Capitol Building, completed in 1888 and modeled after the national Capitol, is located near the center of Austin.

83 The Governor's Mansion has been the home of Texas state governors since 1855. The building itself is a combination of Greek and Southern styles and houses interesting artifacts such as the Sam Houston bed and the Stephen Austin desk.

84 The small towns of southwest Texas bridge the gap between the area's present and its frontier past. The Post Office at Luckenbach is a step into the state's past.

85 Although the majority of Texans live in the bigger cities, the geography of the state, as well as its folklore, is dominated by small towns like Luckenbach, 50 miles west of Austin.

86/87 Sunset at Canyon Lake. One of the man-made Highland Lakes that run through the city of Austin, Canyon Lake is a popular site for swimming, boating and fishing.

88 The LBJ Ranch near Johnson City is still in operation. During Lyndon B Johnson's presidency, the Ranch was often referred to as the Texas White House.

89 The town of Bandera still retains the characteristics and flavor of an old frontier town. Rodeos are a living example of the ruggedness for which Texans are famous.

90 Canyon Dam and Reservoir, near New Braunfels on the Guadalupe River. New Braunfels was founded as a German colony in 1845 and still retains traces of German culture.

91 The Pedernales River runs through rugged country in Pedernales Falls State Park, one of the many fine parks in the diverse lands that lie within Texas' broad boundaries.

92/93 The sun reflects on an oil rig in this classic Texas landscape.

94 The scene of the most infamous battle in Texas' history, the Alamo is a majestic site as it glows against the backdrop of the night sky near San Antonio.

95 On a set that was originally built for a John Wayne movie, periodic recreations of the Alamo are staged at Bracketville in honor of the handful of Texans who laid down their lives in the name of independence.

NORTHWEST AND THE PANHANDLE

In northwest Texas and the Panhandle, the land is rugged and wild, often covered by cacti and populated mainly by wildlife of many species. The gently sloping hills that make up central Texas begin to rise into the High Plains to the west, where the Plains reach a height of 4000 feet above sea level before they ascend still higher to form the southern spur of the Rocky Mountains.

In this western part of Texas, where the Rio Grande makes a 90-degree turn along the Mexican border, are two national parks—Big Bend and Guadalupe Mountains—which contain some of the state's most impressive geographical features and a wide variety of plant and animal life. Big Bend has unmatched fossil and geologic records of the region's formation, while the Guadalupe Mountains claim the highest peak in Texas, at 8751 feet. The Panhandle, which protrudes north between Oklahoma and New Mexico, is part of one of the continent's major geographical features— the Great Plains.

Although winters can be severe, and snow may even fall in this part of the state, the region does not receive much rainfall. Without the use of irrigation and other dry-farming techniques, the land would be unarable. Now, especially in the Panhandle, wheat and sorghum harvests have been bountiful, and the grassy plains support sheep, goats, and cattle. The Panhandle also has tremendous stores of natural gas and helium. In fact, Texas' helium reserves are the most abundant in the world. Throughout this region, cattle and small-scale farming are mainstays of the sparse population.

While most of the land is rural, larger towns and cities such as Abilene, Lubbock, Amarillo, and El Paso flourish whiie retaining the flavor of their origins as frontier towns. Amarillo is a big cattle town and holds one of the world's largest cattle auctions every year. El Paso, the biggest city in the region, exemplifies the strong ties between Texas and Mexico. In fact, El Paso and the Mexican town of Ciudad Juarez, across the Rio Grande, were one city until 1848. The region's pioneer past is recalled by such sites as Fort Bliss, Fort Davis, and the Tigua Indian Reservation—a living testament to the first people of this land.

97 A raft enters Boquillas Canyon in Big Bend National Park. Diverse wildlife and a rich geologic record make the park popular among campers and nature enthusiasts.

98/99 The image of the cowboy has been a large part of Texas' legend since the days of Spanish rule.

100 Although the Longhorn has essentially given way to more modern breeds of cattle, its sturdiness was well-suited to the long drives of the nineteenth century and helped make Texas a great ranching center.

101 Horses trot freely in a grassy field. An indispensable tool of the cowboy, horses have played a major role in the shaping of the state.

102/103 Railroad tracks and telephone lines traverse a drought-stricken area of northern Texas in June 1988.

104 The statue of Buddy Holly in Lubbock, the legendary singer's home town.

105 *The bizarre and wonderful Cadillac Ranch, on Route 66 near Amarillo.*

106 Two Mexicans enjoy the shade of this rock canyon on the Mexican border near El Paso. Spectacular geographic features like this one are common along the border.

107 The home of Judge Roy Bean, "the Law West of the Pecos." The often wild and unorthodox decisions of the Justice of the Peace of Lantry typified frontier justice during the 1800s.

108/109 Pine Spring Canyon in Guadalupe Mountains National Park. One of Texas' two national parks, it boasts the state's highest peak at 8751 feet.

110 Influences from across the border in this part of Texas include the art of bullfighting.

111 Young Tigua Indians of Ysleta del Sur Pueblo perform the traditional Butterfly Dance. Indians, the first inhabitants of Texas, have always played an important role in the culture and history of the state.

112/113 The Prairie Dog Town fork of the Red River at Palo Duro Canyon State Park, southeast of Amarillo.

114/115 Downtown El Paso, with Ciudad Juarez, Mexico in the background. The Rio Grande separates the two cities.

116 The Spanish influence is evident in the architectural style of the New Library at the University of Texas at El Paso.

117 The El Paso Civic Center is a striking combination of Mexican and American influences which reflects the interaction of old and new as well as the many cultures that exist within "the International City."

118 Seen here through the Pinyon Ghost, the sharp peaks of the southern Chisos Mountains dominate the southern section of Big Bend National Park.

119 Horses have always been the preferred mode of transportation in Texas. Here, they allow tourists to take a closer look at the Chisos Mountains.

120/121 This prickly pear cactus in Big Bend is characteristic of the desert plant life that grows in semi-arid West Texas.

122 Santa Elena Canyon, a chasm straddling the
Rio Grande, is one of Big Bend's more remarkable
natural wonders.

123 Big Bend as seen from Mexico, across the
arc of the Rio Grande.

124 Until Indian troubles subsided in the 1880s, Fort Davis was a U.S. Cavalry outpost engaged in protecting settlers from the hostile Comanches and Apaches. Today it is a national historic site.

125 Near Fort Davis, the William J McDonald Astronomical Observatory on Mount Locke serves as a facility of the University of Texas. Its telescope, at 107 inches, is the fifteenth largest of its kind in the world.

126/127 The setting sun appears from behind a cloud in the big sky over an area of rich Texas farmland.